HOW TO KILL YOUR GHOSTS

POEMS BY
ROWAN GLADISH

AOS PUBLISHING, 2024
AOS POETRY, 2024
Copyright © 2024 Rowan Gladish
All rights reserved under International and Pan-American copyright conventions.
ISBN: 978-1-990496-22-6

Cover Design: Lex Rose

Visit AOS Publishing's website:
www.aospublishing.com

DENIAL

HAUNTED

I can touch
the calluses on your fingertips
hold your body in my arms
as it shakes
but no tears come

I can feel
the sorrow of mourning
even though you're still here
I know as I sleep next to you
I sleep in a grave

I believe in ghosts
and I live in a haunted house
you know it too
as you drift through the halls
unable to move on

NEVER ABLE TO R.I.P.

You're lying in the ground
And I'm digging my way down
Trying to find a way to stay
By your side and waste away

When I say
That I am feeling anxious
What I mean is that
My stomach has taken
What is left of its lining and
Twisted it into knots
Cajoled my legs into shaking
So hard I can barely walk
Forced the ocean that
Lives ever present
Behind my eyes to rise above
Ground level and crest over

When I say
That I am feeling anxious
I can only seem to make anyone understand
If I describe it like romanticized
Butterflies in my stomach
And they dismiss it as the pitiful turmoil
Of youthful melodrama
And I smile and force
My legs to stop shaking
The ocean to leave with the tide
And say "never mind" still feeling
The threat of knots in my stomach

- A battle I fight every day

I want to be
Tough
Confident
Scary
Strong
But the pile of dishes
Building in my sink
Is still enough to unravel me
Even on my best days

- I wish I knew the better version of myself

WHICH BOOK SHOULD I READ?

Some days
My house becomes
A bookshelf and I
Am left in the center
With half read pages
Covering every surface
Desperate to escape
Whatever real life means
But so frozen in indecision
That I can never get past
The first page
Of anything

You were behind the wheel
When you said to me
"Isn't it crazy
That I could just
Drive off the road?"
And I wasn't scared
But maybe I should have been

- Too naive to see the danger

THE ME WHO DOESN'T EXIST

How odd it is
that we don't bury
the people we used to be.
No way to mourn
the us we lost
at least not formally.

I often wonder
if she would be proud
of who I turned out to be.
Honestly I don't think
the past versions of myself
would care at all for me.

She never would have thought
that I would be so cold
that I would never see all of her friends.
But she's gone, unburied, forgotten
she never really existed
or at least I can pretend.

And then she's there
somewhere in the future
where I am nobody.
I wonder if I'd
be proud of her
or if she misses me.

Look maybe I'm not
Supposed to know
What I'm doing
Maybe it's the world
That's fucked up
Instead of me

- I can't always be to blame

CONTROL

You used to breathe
The air from my lungs
And I would wait
Suffocating
Until you were ready
To give it back

DEAR DIARY

There's nothing quite like an empty journal
Even though I never get around to writing in them
When I first pick them up I can't help but think
That maybe if I fill every page
My thoughts will stop trying to trick my brain
Into thinking that breathing and drowning are the same thing
And maybe I'll be able to sleep at night
If I can somehow transfer out the memory
Of being laughed at in the second grade
By a faceless figure whose name I can't remember
Maybe if I wrote down my stream of consciousness
I'd be able to decipher secret messages
Morse code tapping on the inside of my skull
Telling me exactly when and how I'm going to die
A new journal always holds the promise
Of letting go of the weight carried on the crown of my head
Letting it fall into ink and paper
Far away from me
But never too far to retrieve
There's nothing quite like an empty journal
I've built up a collection
Of promised solutions in pretty blank pages
That I never ever fill

EMPTY

No
I would say
I'm not in the mood
I would say
I'm too tired
I would say
Because somehow *I don't want to* was never enough.
                                        Please
                                    You would say
                            Don't you love me?
                                      You would say
                         Why won't you prove it?
                            Your hands would wander
                                  always moving down
          no matter how many times I pushed them away.

I learned very quickly
                        The consequences of resisting you.
Never any violence, never any force
                            A turn followed by silence.
                            You would face away from me.

I'm sorry
I would say

                              I'm just disappointed
                                    You would mutter.
                                        I'm horrible
                                        You would say
                            No one should love me

I love you
I would say
But now I was desperate to prove it.

I told myself
That I wanted this
I forced myself
> To move with your rhythm
> To sound how you wanted me to sound
> To be what you wanted me to be

I told myself
That I asked for this
Even after all the times
I said no.

Lying there
Unmoving
I always felt empty
As if I had given up a part of myself to you
And now I wanted it back.
> You would turn away from me
> And put on your clothes.
> Turn on your phone.
> You got what you wanted
> And suddenly

I was no longer interesting.

You are gone now
And I am with someone new
For the first time in years.
We are kissing
I am lying in his bed
And suddenly I am filled with fear
> Your voice is in my head
> **He will want more from you.**

I don't want to feel empty again.

I'm sorry
I say
And I am crying
"For what?"
He asks
And moves to hold me, gentle and secure
I tell him
That I can't give him what he wants
I tell him
I'm sorry
That I can't be enough
I'm sorry
Please don't let me go
I'm sorry
Please don't turn away
I'm sorry
His arms stay around me
And I am confused
I don't know what happens next.
I look up
And he is crying too
"I'm so sorry"
He says
"That he hurt you like that"

FOR YOU

i always knew i was small.
You loved me for it.
You loved it for me.
You loved it for You.

Did I ever really know you?
Or was the person I fell in love with
Just another one
Of your beautiful lies?

- I guess you fooled me

IMMORTALIZED

Do you think if I

Drink enough whiskey
Write enough poems
Spend enough sleepless nights
Cry enough oceans

I'll eventually forget
All about you?

TO ALL MY LONG LOST RELATIVES

Family is weird
and hard to define.
Just because
we're connected by blood
does that really group us together?
To choose a favourite relative
feels like picking an acquaintance.
Looking at an instagram life and saying
I'd like to know you better.
There are dozens of people who have my nose
my cheekbones, my eyes
who I don't know at all.
Maybe in a different place or a different time
we'd all have Sunday dinners
at one long table.
But here and now
I'll double tap a heart
to let you know
I'm thinking of you.

GRIND CULTURE

Everyone is so focused
on growth
and it's important
to cultivate your garden.
Pull out the weeds.
Water the plants.
Re-pot the seedlings.
But don't forget why
you're building in the first place.
If you never stop to smell the flowers
you'll always feel like
there aren't any.

People always say
Never forget where you've been
Never forget who you are
But what if I
Don't want to remember
How I became me?

What if instead
Of remembering strength
All I can see is pain?

What if who I am
Is built on shaky foundations?

What if I
Don't want to find out?

What if I
Want to disappear?

- Sometimes I wish I never met me

LEFTOVERS

Maybe my mind
is sort of like my fridge
the leftovers just pile up
and I keep adding more
even though I know
I'll never eat them
Still for some reason
I feel so guilty when
I try to throw them out

Maybe this is why
I can never let anything go

ANOTHER PANDEMIC DISCOVERY

I always fancied myself
an introvert but since I've been given
the chance to be alone
for two long years
I'm realizing that maybe I've been
an extrovert all along and
without my charger of social interaction
my battery is slowly running out

Let me drink
From the mouth of Dionysus
Whether it is wine or madness
I could never tell
But what does it really matter
As long as it gives me
Relief

- I promise I don't have a problem

ALREADY LOST TO HISTORY

I wonder if I'm part
of the last generation
to cherish their first CD.

Here is a part of who I am
held so delicately in my hands
so breakable and yet
so important to me.

I can still remember
the childlike wonder
of possessing my anthem.

Playing it over and over
on my CD player alarm clock.
Do kids even have those anymore?

Is this what it feels like
to grow old?

I feel it
in every coffee you bring me
going out of your way every morning.
I know it
everytime our arms
graze against each other
and linger just a little too long.
I can practically hear it
when you drop everything just to make sure
I'm feeling okay.
But please don't tell me.
Not yet.
Not until I'm sure
that I'm ready to accept it.
Because you deserve more than
"it's not the right time"
and I want to be the one
who gives that to you.
So don't tell me yet.
Just wait a bit longer
until I can gather the courage
to say it back.

- I know you love me/I know I love you

ANGER

I'm still wide awake
At 2 am
When am I supposed
To outgrow this pain

- Shouldn't I be happy by now?

THE REST OF YOUR LIFE

For a moment I thought
that I would spend the rest of my life
chasing you.

But the moment passed and it suddenly became clear
that while I loved you
you were killing me.

And even though I know I shouldn't wish ill
I hope you feel
hurt
sad
alone.
I hope you spend the rest of your life
regretting the way you treated me.

BETTER

How was I
Supposed to know
What better looked like
When you were all
I ever had

No one ever told me
That sex is supposed to be
For me
About me
And only if
I
Want
It.

- A woman is always an object before she is a person

LEARNING FORGIVENESS

The problem isn't
That I can't forgive you
For what you did to me
The problem is
That I can't forgive me
For letting it happen

When we were together
The girl I was promised
To love you forever
And she kept that promise
The girl I was loved you
Right up until the moment she died

- At least one of us was honest

If nothing else
You could have done me the courtesy
Of mourning the girl you killed

- Did I mean anything to you?

To the younger me:
I'm sorry that you didn't know better.
To the older me:
I'm sorry that you do.

- Duality

I COME WITH A CONTRACT NOW

Unconditional love
is a privilege
that should be felt
only by a parent
for their child

Unconditional love
in a romantic relationship
is a trap
When they say "do you love me unconditionally"
what they mean is "how much will you take before
walking away"

And so I love you conditionally

Terms as follows:

1. Respect me
2. Work to gain and keep trust
3. Communicate as best you can
4. Never knowingly break my heart

Will you accept?

Please sign on the the line below:
x_____

I'm so tired of trying
To make what you did to me
Sound poetic

- You don't deserve to be made beautiful

VENGEFUL SPIRITS

I wanted to be
Immutable in your mind.
The blaring alarm
Causing you panic every morning.
The screeching eagles
To your Prometheus.
I wanted you to fear
The sound of my voice
And I wanted to scream
At every corner you turned.
But the only justice
I was able to find for myself
Was to stay silent and fade
Away like a ghost
Unsure if I ever really got
To haunt you.

You were my sun
And you used to call
Me moonlight
I remember how
Your smile
Would light up
Any room
I remember how
I held your
Shaking shoulders
On harder days
I remember all
Our promises
Pinkies crossed
Do you remember?
Or am I the only one
Stuck with this pain?

- It doesn't seem fair

You let me know that
If I couldn't have you
Then someone else would
But if you didn't want me
Then no one else could

- Turns out, I want me anyway

"Love yourself" they cry
but somehow every facet
of my body
is an affront
an imperfection
a sin

How can you cry
"love yourself"
while you market products
that cover every
miniscule bump

How can you cry
"love yourself"
and force a weight loss
pill and regime
down my throat

What society
have we created
where showing a natural body
has become
an act of rebellion

- Positivity is misogyny's new favourite tool

SOMETIMES TRAUMA LASTS A LIFETIME

I am confused about sex again
Unsure if I'm doing what I want
Or what I think he wants from me
And I'm losing track of the years
That it's been since I was with you
But still this lingering thing
That I have never found a name for
Is haunting me
I guess I'll call it trauma
I hate how even when
He assures me that
The second I'm uncomfortable
All he wants from me
Is a hug
I still worry that
If I don't do what
You taught me I was supposed to
When I'm supposed to
He'll be so angry
So sad
That I will have to dissolve
To appease him
And I love that
He's nothing like you
And he would never
Could never
Hurt me in that way
Or any other
But I hate that
I forget you for days
For weeks
For months
Just to have your angry voice
In my head
When I go to bed

Trying to be better
And walking away
Instead of doing everything I could
To make you hurt
Like you hurt me
Was the hardest thing
I ever had to do

- You should be fucking thankful

I want to kiss you
So violently
That it kills every sad thought
Either of us could have

- Love prevails

BARGAINING

THE PROCESS OF MOVING ON

I don't know anymore
If I'm trying to remember you
Or forget you

I don't know which
Is worse

I wish I had ended it sooner
Instead of spending years trying to fix
What was always broken beyond repair

Maybe then I could have thought of you
As my first love
Now when I think of you
All I remember is pain

- You were supposed to be nostalgia, not nightmares

Things that google can't answer for me:

1. Why can't I let go?
2. Why are all my shower conversations with you?
3. How do you still hurt me?
4. Why do I let you?

- Some answers only come with time

When I kissed you
On a dare
I rationalized
That it was all for fun
And ignored how I
Had jumped at the chance

- I kissed a girl and I liked it

CEMETERY WALKS

When I was 15
I didn't think that I
Would make it this far
And for some reason
That didn't bother me much then
But now I live in constant fear
That I won't make it any further
That time will wash me away
And everything will have meant nothing
And so I spend every moment
Trying to leave a permanent mark
Hoping someone will find my name one day
And wonder who I was

Sometimes I like to visit old cemeteries
And lovingly trace the names of strangers
On worn down tombstones
I read the description and for a moment
I almost miss these strangers
From 100 years ago
I mourn for "beloved father and husband", for "loved child" for "sister and friend"
I guess I just hope that one day
Someone will take a moment to mourn for me too
To ensure that my life
Was more than just dust
Blown away into nothing
When it ended

SCALES AND I NEVER GET ALONG

The relationship I have
With exercise is so complex
I know I should do it
For my health and happiness
But I can only manage to fit it in
When I've been obsessing
Over weight and beauty
And so I feel such strong
Cognitive dissonance every time
I step on a treadmill because
I know that the goals
I'm trying to reach are just
Arbitrary numbers created
By the patriarchy and meant
To please men and sexualize
Women and I'm a feminist I
Promise but somehow all
That shit still weighs
Me down

FRIENEMY

Why can I believe
That all bodies are beautiful
Except the one
That gifts me life

Maybe one day
My body and I will reconcile
And I will apologize
For all my mistreatment
And thank her
For all her nourishment

You said that you just wanted
Me to be happy
And I know that was a lie

But I wish that you could see
How happy I've been
Since I left you

Too bad I blocked you
You don't deserve
The validation anyways

- Even a broken clock is right twice a day

The very nature
Of living
Is so limiting
So finite
I can't decide which
Of the billion things
That exist
I should do
Before I die
So I sit here
And ponder
And panic
And do
None of them

- Anxious thoughts again

ON GETTING OLD

I never understood people
Who said they wanted to die
before they're old

I can't believe that you would rather exist
in the fantasy of neverending youth
instead of welcoming the next adventure.

ON GETTING OLD: BLACKOUT POEM

I never understood people
who ▇▇▇ wanted to die
▇▇▇▇▇

I ▇▇▇▇▇▇ would rather exist
in the fantasy of neverending ▇▇
▇▇▇▇▇▇▇▇▇

Nothing was worse for my self esteem
Than watching my Mother
Diet and complain
Unhappy
Unhappy
Unhappy
Now I cry tears of fear
Every little pound I gain
Afraid of being
Unhappy
Unhappy
Unhappy

- I always thought you were beautiful Mom

My favourite foods are
Ice cream
Mac n' cheese
Cheesecake
Chocolate milk
And when I was 12
I realized I was lactose intolerant
So I guess the point is
Enjoy what you have
While you have it

- Everything is temporary

I hate the cliché
Of "you complete me"
You don't
You could never
Because I was already whole
Before you met me
I could have done it all alone
All my life
But ever since meeting you
I've never once wanted to

- You are a choice, not a necessity

BELONGING TO ME

I hate most parts
Of getting older
But I love that
Some of me is changed

It's just so wonderful
To know that there
Are parts of me
You've never seen

The more I change
The more I feel like myself
Instead of your
Discarded property

NO MORE STAPLES

There are no more staples.
And I am crying
even though the project
isn't due for a week
and the dollar store is right
down the street.
There are no more staples.
But also, there's no more time.
Why do I feel like I left
my youth behind
when I'm still so young?
There are no more staples.
But that really isn't the point.
Why do stupid jokes
I made in middle school that
no one remembers still
keep me up at night?
There are no more staples.
The fridge broke down
last week and I
can't afford savings so
now my credit is
all maxed out.
There are no more staples.
I don't know if I've
ever really felt closure
all my past relationships
friends or lovers have
always just ended.
There are no more staples.
Why don't I ever have
any energy when
all I do is sleep
why do I always
wake up so tired?
There are no more staples.
And I am spiralling
into my box of bad things

I usually keep locked
away in my mind
out of sight at least.
There are no more staples.
But the project isn't due
for a week and the dollar store
is just down the street so I
take a deep breath and
go to get my coat.

YOUNG LOVE

We could have been high school sweethearts
Everyone's perfect romance story
Each other's first and last love.

We could have been high school sweethearts
Uncomfortably married by 20
Never knowing anyone but each other.

We could have been high school sweethearts
Miserable by 30 and hating each other
But too scared to start over.

We could have been high school sweethearts
But instead you were my worst heartbreak.

Thank you.

WORTH

I am worthy
Of the love I give
I am not asking
You to provide it
I am warning you
That I will find it

Sometimes your lips
Are drowning me
While your hands
Drag me from the ocean
Onto dry land

- This is my favourite type of purgatory

DEPRESSION

HOW TO KILL YOUR GHOST

In the mornings
When I make my coffee
I feel your breath
On the back of my neck.

In my rearview mirror
As I drive to work
I catch just a glance
Of your cold eyes.

On my lunch break
Your text tone rings
On someone elses phone
And I flinch.

In the evenings
The TV blares unending
But it can never drown out
The sound of your voice.

At midnight
I wake up in
A cold sweat and feel
Your arms around me.

Tightening until
I can barely breathe
Smothering me
Never letting go.

You whisper that
I will always be yours
You will follow me to
My grave.

It's just a moment though
And then I'm alone

Heart beating so fast
I'm sure it will burst.

The ghost of you
Is haunting me
I know you're long gone
But you never really left.

But I don't haunt you
You moved on
And I did too
I'm happy.

So why do these scars
Feel like fresh wounds
Why does every voice
Sound like you.

Someday I'll learn
How to kill your ghost
And maybe finally alone
I won't feel so lonely.

A COLLECTION OF BROKEN HEARTS

A boy once told me
That he was in love with me
But I knew that he was really
In love with kindness
And I had been the first
To show it in awhile

I wonder if he's
Still searching for salvation
We don't talk anymore
But I hope he stopped
Searching for the minimum
And found the love he deserved

My mother told me
Don't lose yourself
Not in a friend
Or a sibling
Or a man

But I lose myself
Over and over
In my childhood best friend's
Brace filled smile

In the disapproving gaze
Of the never appeased
Always longing
Never proud

In his hands
On darker nights
When I felt I wanted
To feel nothing

Sometimes I think
My mother was really saying
Do not make my mistakes
Make sure you never lose yourself
In a child

- I'm sorry I stole your life away

PIECES TO PIECES

I am the chips fallen off all the stones I've loved,
and all the stones who have loved me.
I am beginning to understand the meaning of impact on
a soul.
I write my y's like my best friend from middle school,
even though she's hated me for years.
Everytime I see a comedy show I think of the funny boy
I crushed on in 7th grade.
I have my taste in music from someone whose name I've
nearly forgotten.
I like the drinks an ex first showed me.
I am made from pieces of people I will never see again.
I wonder how many pieces of me they took with them
when we parted.

OLDER

I never really grasped
That I will grow older
And every time I have
I've mourned the moments
Wasted

FAMINE

You kissed me
And your eyes
Were hungry
I thought that meant
You craved me
And if you were hungry
For me
I was starving
For love

But sometimes hunger
Is cavernous
Never ending
Taking and taking and taking
Until there's nothing left
Even as you
Picked my bones clean
I was so happy
Just to be wanted

FEELING S.A.D.

My mood swings
With the seasons
In summer's light
I think that maybe
I've finally been fixed
But winter illuminates
The cracks in my skin
And every spring I have
To start again.

I keep getting older
But I never seem to be
Any less lost

- Wasn't age supposed to make me wise?

These days I worry
That all my best stories
Are already behind me
And when the time comes
I won't have anyone
To reminisce with

- I miss my childhood friends

WHAT DID WE EVEN HAVE?

When it was over
I thought I would be sad
But all I felt was relief

What was I supposed
To do with that
After so many years

Of holding on to

N
O
T
H
I
N
G

FRIENDS CAN BREAK YOUR HEART TOO

Don't you remember
Creating secret languages
Writing notes that only we could read
Don't you remember
Staying up till 3 am
Telling each other stories
Passing out on your bedroom floor
Don't you remember
Picking daisies together
Weaving them into crowns
Becoming our own queens

Of all the heartbreak I've faced
You broke me the worst
All my summer nights are spent
Remembering you.

GEN Z ANTHEM

I never knew
There were so many ways to be tired.
No,
Exhausted.

Sometimes I wish
That I could pull you into myself
Use my bones as a barrier
To protect you from the world
Keep you locked behind
My ribcage where I know
You'd feel at home
After all you've owned
My heart for longer
Than I ever could have guessed

- Do you think I could be home to you?

I wish that I
Could take your pain
Could draw it from your lips
And swallow it.
I'd rather walk
On a bed of nails
Than watch you get
A paper cut.

- But I know you'd never let me

ACCEPTANCE

LOSING YOU

In losing you, I lost a part of myself.
I lost the knowledge that I was loved, I lost the security and strength lent to me, I lost the ability to trust kindly and love fully.
In losing you, I lost a friend.
I lost the one who you stole away before you even left, I lost the ones I couldn't face without you by my side.
In losing you, I lost my future.
I lost my plans, built so carefully to please you.
In losing you, I lost my ambitions.
Designed around supporting you.

Losing you felt as though the world was crashing down around me, as though the sun had exploded and somehow only I was feeling the backlash.
Losing you made me feel scared.
Alone.
Pointless.
It made me feel angry that I had wasted all my time.
I felt
Used.
Unloveable.
Unwanted.
Unneeded.
Unimportant.
Useless.

But all of the hurt was worth it.
In losing you, I found him.
Losing you taught me what real love is.
What real care is.
What real trust is.
Losing you left me with scars that you would have called ugly,
But he tells me they're beautiful.

I would lose you again,
And again,
And again
If it meant I could be where I am now.
Who I am now.
With him, like I am now.

Losing you absolutely destroyed me.
And it gave me the chance to rebuild bigger, better, and stronger
Over the ashes of who I used to be.

When it comes to death
There's nothing I can do
But wait

- What's the point in worrying about an inevitability?

Sometimes I think
We get so caught up
In what we experience
That our sense of what is normal
What is okay
Is skewed

And occasionally it takes
Someone barging in
Knocking down your walls and shaking you
To realize that what you had before
Was never something to strive for

- What you gave me was never love

We got together so young
That every glaring flaw I saw
I reasoned you would outgrow

It turns out that I
Simply outgrew you

- Darling, growth is a beautiful colour on me

I told myself
That you'd be back
In 2 weeks
6 months
A year
But the seasons came and went
And it didn't take long for me
To realize
That the girl who wanted you
Left when you did

- Please forget my number

We are all
Going to die someday
On my worst days
This deflates me
On my best
It's the reason for everything

- What does life mean without the promise of death?

I used to hate
the girl you left me for
but now instead
of blaming your next victim
I just hope that I'm
the last one you break

- Only one of you made a promise

MY BODY IS JUST A PLACEHOLDER FOR A COFFIN

God I am so tired
Of trying to decipher
What my body means to me.
Is she a goddess
Or an enemy?
Should I treat her with kindness
Or contempt?

>   Honestly it's all
>   Bullshit.
>   All my body is
>   Is a precursor
>   To the rot and dust
>   That death will bring.
>
>   Might as well enjoy the ride.

UNOPENED

I used to keep a box
of all our memories
I cherished it for years

You already knew we were over
but when I handed you that box, unopened,
you knew we had ended

DANDELION

I was a dandelion
You would blow
And I would make a wish
As you scattered the pieces of me.

For a while afterwards
I could only picture myself
As the dead empty stem
That you ripped from the ground.

But there is beauty in destruction
And all my wishes came true
As the parts of me you banished
Slowly began to grow.

LOVE IS SUPPOSED TO BE EASY

I thought I knew love
I thought that it was built
On eggshells
That I had to walk on
Without breaking
But our love
Was so easy
We ran in
Reckless and free
And I kept waiting
For the consequences
But they never came

I have become my own light before
And when I am left alone in the dark
I remember how to shine again

- No one can ever extinguish me

SOMEONE NEW

I am wanting for what I cannot have
I am fighting for what I cannot have
I am pushing for what I cannot have
I am hurting for what I cannot have
I am tearing myself apart, piece by piece, for what I cannot have, for what I can never have, for what I never had to begin with –
And then I am awake
You are breathing softly, slowing my heartbeat. Your arms are around me, instinctively pulling me closer even in sleep, sensing my discomfort and protecting me in a way I have never been protected.
For one horrible horrible moment I believe that I cannot have you.
For a few painful seconds I see you walking away, I see you happy without me, I think I couldn't possibly deserve you.
I always think I couldn't possibly deserve you.
Suddenly, I am past wanting what I cannot have.
I am wanting what I shouldn't have.
I couldn't possibly be enough to deserve this.
It's hard to navigate life with you. So different from what I know. So different from what I've become accustomed to.
Your affection is overwhelming, a force I've never felt directed at me before and yet I never want it to stop.
You tell me I'm important.
You tell me I'm loved.
You tell me you'll stay.
It's entirely my fault that I can never fully believe you.
You are everything I have ever needed.
I have become accustomed to being told that I am never enough.
I know that I am never enough, that I never was enough, that I can never be enough.

I am always on edge, always knowing that any minute now, you will demand that I tear what's left of me away to keep you, always knowing that I will helplessly oblige if it means I can have you a little longer.
I am always waiting, but the time never comes.
You never demand anything at all from me.
I'm not sure how to show that I love you without giving myself away.
Is it possible that I've been taught to love wrong?
I am scared of being used. So very scared of letting myself be taken over just to please, even for a moment, just to feel useful.
And yet I am scared that you refuse to use me.
How much longer will you want me if you want nothing from me?
How much longer will you love me if you never get to use me?
You are still sleeping, but starting to wake up.
I ban the thoughts from my mind, and let the pure goodness that is you fill it instead.
I am learning, all over again, how to love.
You are teaching me.
I trust that you'll teach me right.

Every time I'm drunk
I want to peel back my skin
Show you all the dark parts of myself
Show you all the traumatizing things
That happened to me
Make you see
As if you were there.
But you weren't there
You were here
Waiting for me
For this version of me
Who's ready to be loved
By you.

- Sometimes timing is everything

If all the hurt
Led me here to you
There's nothing I wouldn't do
Over again

- The first of many love songs

SPEECHLESS

I'm sorry
That I haven't written
Enough love poems
About you

I think maybe
You're the one thing
That could ever leave me
Speechless

FOREVER

You said
"I love you"
And suddenly
Forever was
Such an easy
Promise to make

Now I know
What it was all for
It was for now
This moment
This second
This piece of happiness
We've built together

- And it was all worth it

WHEN THEY SAY LOVE IS BLIND

I don't mind
Running in blind
As long as it's your hand
That's leading me

When we met
You stopped smoking
Even though I never asked
Just because you hated
Seeing my disappointment
I don't think I've ever been
Treated so gently before

- I never had to ask if you loved me

PEACE

I can't remember
What your voice sounds like
What your favourite colour is
What song you always pick
When given the chance
I can finally
Breathe.

- Healing

NO MORE NIGHTMARES

After all our years together
I thought it would be impossible
To disentangle you from my life

But I packed a couple boxes
Burned a few things
And hit block wherever I could

And now it's almost like
It never really happened
And you were just a bad dream

BURNED BRIDGES

We were ziplining
and you cut the cable
at first I was terrified
and then I enjoyed the fall
before I was caught by a net
and moved on with my life

SOULMATES

We've been here before
In whatever life was first
And we'll be here again
In whatever life comes next

PAPER FLOWERS

I'll build you a thousand palaces
To hold all your dreams
And I'll give you a thousand
Paper flowers
To remind you of me

When your fingers reached inside me
It felt like you were burrowing
Making yourself a home
Out of my body

- I was more than willing to welcome you

TO BE LOVED: PART ONE

I wake up to find
That I am
      H
       E
        A
         V
          I
           E
           R
Than the day before
And I tell him
That I am sorry.
He gets on his knees
Places soft kisses on
My stomach
My thighs
My arms
And says
"Don't apologize love,
for enjoying the meals
I make for you."

TO BE LOVED: PART TWO

I tell him
That I feel
C O M B U S T I B L E
Like the gas has been
Left on at the stove
And any minute now
An unsuspecting Victim
Will walk in and light a cigarette
He says
"Dont worry love,
I'll always check the stove,
And I promise I'll never be
A smoker."

When I moved in with you
On my first visit home
My father asked me
Between our normal jokes
If I was happy
And for the first time
I answered honestly

- Yes

Wake me up
My darling
Before the the dream gets cold
And I remember
That I'm growing old
Leave me with a hazy memory
Of your smile in the sun
And then remind me
What it means to be young

- How I would choose to spend my last days

LEARNING LOVE LANGUAGES

When you say
I thought you would like this
I got this for you
I made you a coffee
I did the dishes
Don't worry, I've got this
All I hear is
I love you
I love you
I love you
I love you
I love you

I could fill a hundred romance books
Writing about
The quiet saturday nights
We share together

- We are the greatest romance I ever read

KISSING IN THE RAIN IS OVERRATED

The movies all show
A kiss in the rain
But for us it was more
About running through the downpour
As lightning painted the sky
And the thunder left us deaf
Only to collapse
Soaking wet and laughing
In the front hallway
Of our safe home

HAPPINESS WILL COME

It's the little things
Reading a book
Sipping warm apple cinnamon tea
It tastes like early fall
Even in the middle of January
A pine scented candle is glowing
And I can hear the comforting drum
Of you in the shower upstairs
I find that I am smiling
And realize that I really am happy

GIVE AND TAKE

I am drunk
And making the bed at 1 am
So you don't have to

We both know that tomorrow
It will be your turn
To take care of me

I never knew the freedom
That love could provide
Until this moment

When my name
First came from your mouth
I felt ethereal
And knew that it didn't
Belong to me anymore

- I am yours, fully and forever

ADDITIONAL NOTES & CREDITS

"The Me Who Doesn't Exist" has previously appeared on *The Pittsburgher*

"Empty" has previously appeared on *The Catalyst View*

"How to Kill Your Ghost" has previously appeared in *Forget Me Not Press*

"Someone New" has previously appeared in *Wandering Autumn Magazine*

Printed in the USA
CPSIA information can be obtained
at www.ICGtesting.com
LVHW010858190324
774815LV00007B/148